Complete Works for
Piano Four Hands

Opp. 66, 85, 109, 130

Edited by Alfred Dörffel

Robert Schumann

DOVER PUBLICATIONS, INC.
Mineola, New York

Copyright

Published in Canada by General Publishing Company, Ltd., 895 Don Mills Road, 400-2 Park Centre, Toronto, Ontario M3C 1W3.
Published in the United Kingdom by David & Charles, Brunel House, Forde Close, Newton Abbot, Devon TQ12 4PU.

Bibliographical Note

This Dover edition, first published in 2001, is an unabridged republication of an authoritative early edition. The annotated contents list and glossary are newly added, and English titles have replaced the original German titles in the music.

International Standard Book Number: 0-486-41889-8

Manufactured in the United States of America
Dover Publications, Inc., 31 East 2nd Street, Mineola, N.Y. 11501

Contents

5/09

Glossary of German Terms in the Music

(capitalizations given as they appear in the scores)

Ausdrucksvoll und sehr gehalten, expressive and very sustained

Belebt, doch nicht zu rasch, lively but not too fast

Einfach, simply *(semplice)*
Erstes Tempo = *Tempo I*
Etwas langsamer, somewhat slower
Etwas lebhafter, somewhat livelier
Etwas zurückhaltend, holding back a little

Festlich, festive

Immer schwächer und schwächer, fading away more and more
Im Tempo = *a tempo*
Im Volkston, like a folksong

Langsam und gemessen, slow and measured
Lebhaft (nicht zu schnell), lively (not too fast)

markiert = *marcato*
Mäßiges Tempo, moderate tempo
Mit Verschiebung, with the "soft" pedal
Munter, cheerfully

Nach und nach etwas belebter, gradually somewhat more animated
Nach und nach schwächer, gradually fading away
Nicht schnell, not fast
  etwas gravitätisch, somewhat pompously (gravely)
  feierlich, with pomp and solemnity
  und sehr gesangvoll zu spielen, and to be played *molto cantabile*
Nicht zu schnell, not too fast
Noch schneller, faster yet

Rechte, right hand
Reuig, andächtig, with contrition and piety

Sehr kräftig, very powerfully
Sehr markiert = *molto marcato*
Schnell / Schneller, fast / faster
So schnell als möglich, as fast as possible

Ziemlich rasch, rather fast
Ziemlich schnell, rather fast

Complete Works for
Piano Four Hands
Opp. 66, 85, 109, 130

To Lida Bendemann neé Schadow

Pictures from the East

6 Impromptus, Op. 66 (1848)

To Lida Bendemann neé Schadow

Pictures from the East

6 Impromptus, Op. 66 (1848)

sf
p
Ped. * Ped. * Ped. * Ped. *
B
p
fp
dim.
C
Etwas langsamer
Im Tempo
fp
D
2

B
C
Etwas langsamer
Im Tempo
D
dim.

p
E
cresc.
sf
sf
sf
F
sf
sf
sf
sf
p
G
cresc.
sf
sf
sf
sf
sf
sf
sf
sf
sf
f
f

E
p
cresc.
sf
sf
sf
F
sf
sf
sf
sf
p
G
cresc.
sf
sf
sf
sf
sf
sf
sf
sf
sf
8
f
f

Nicht schnell und sehr gesangvoll zu spielen
2.
p
f
fp
fp
p
1.
2.
p
sf
p
p
dimin.
Ped.

Nicht schnell und sehr gesangvoll zu spielen
2.
p
f
fp
1.
2.
sf
dim.

3.
Im Volkston
ff
Etwas lebhafter
mf
A
p
Etwas langsamer.
p
Im Tempo
cresc.
f
sf
sf
sf
ff

3.
Im Volkston
ff
Etwas lebhafter.
mf
A
p
Etwas langsamer.
Im Tempo
cresc.
f
sf
ff

CODA Schneller
f
sf
sf
p
ff
p
ff
p
ff
B
Noch schneller
sf
sf
dimin.
C
p
ff
sf
sf
sf
sf
sf
Ped.
Ped.
Ped.
Ped.

CODA
Schneller
f
ff
sf
p
ff
p
ff
p
B
ff
Noch schneller.
f
fp dimin.
fp
C
p
ff
sf
sf
sf
sf
sf
Ped.
Ped.
Ped.
Ped.

Nicht schnell
4.
p
p
p
p
Ped.
Ped.

Nicht schnell
4.
p
fp
Ped.

Lebhaft
5.
p
f
ff
A
sf
B

5.
Lebhaft
A
B

ff sf
sf
f
sf
sf
sf
sf
p
p

ff
f
sf
sf
sf
sf
p
fp
fp
p

C
D
E

C
D
E

Reuig, andächtig
6.
p
dim.
A
fp
fp
fp
tr
tr
B
p
tr
fp
tr
f
fp
Nach und nach etwas belebter
f
p
p

Reuig, andächtig
6.
p
A
dimin.
fp
fp
fp
B
p
fp
f
fp
Nach und nach etwas belebter
f
p
p
p

C
p
crescendo
D
ff
Etwas zurückhaltend
sf
sf
sf
sf
Ped.
Ped.

f
f
C
p
crescendo
sf
sf
D
ff sf
sf
Etwas zurückhaltend
sf
sf
Ped.
Ped.

Erstes Tempo
p
dimin.
p
dimin.
E
ff
sf
sf
sf
sf
sf
sf
sf
F
p
pp
Fine

Erstes Tempo
p
p
dimin.
p
dimin.
E
ff
sf
sf
sf
sf
Ped.
Ped.
Ped.
sf
sf
sf
sf
sf
sf
F
p
pp
Ped.
Ped.
Ped.
Ped.
Ped.
Fine

12 Four-Hand Pieces
for Small and Big Children
Op. 85 (1849)

1. Birthday March

12 Four-Hand Pieces
for Small and Big Children
Op. 85 (1849)

1. Birthday March

2. Bear Dance

2. Bear Dance

3. Garden Melody

3. Garden Melody

4. While Weaving Garlands

4. While Weaving Garlands

p
f
p
fp
f
p
p
p
A
B
1mo
p
p

A
B

5. Croatian March

5. Croatian March

mf
ff
D
sf
sf
ff
sf
sf
mf
sf
sf
mf
E
f
F
f
mf

D
E
F
mf
sf
ff
f

Nach und nach schwächer
G
ff
sf
H
mf
fp
p
I Immer schwächer und
schwächer
pp
1

Nach und nach schwächer
ff
G
sf
sf
sf
sf
mf
H
p
fp
fp
fp
Immer schwächer und schwächer
I
fp
1
pp

6. Sorrow

6. Sorrow

1mo
7. Tournament March
Sehr kräftig

7. Tournament March

Sehr kräftig

A
tr
B
p
C
fp
f

A
B
C
p
f
fp
sf

f
f
tr
sf
tr
D
E
ff
3

f
f
sf
sf
sf
sf
D
E
ff
sf
sf
3
3

8. Round Dance

8. Round Dance

fp
fp
p
Ped.
Ped.
B
Nach und nach
schwächer
C

fp
fp
p
B
Nach und nach schwächer
C

9. By the Fountain

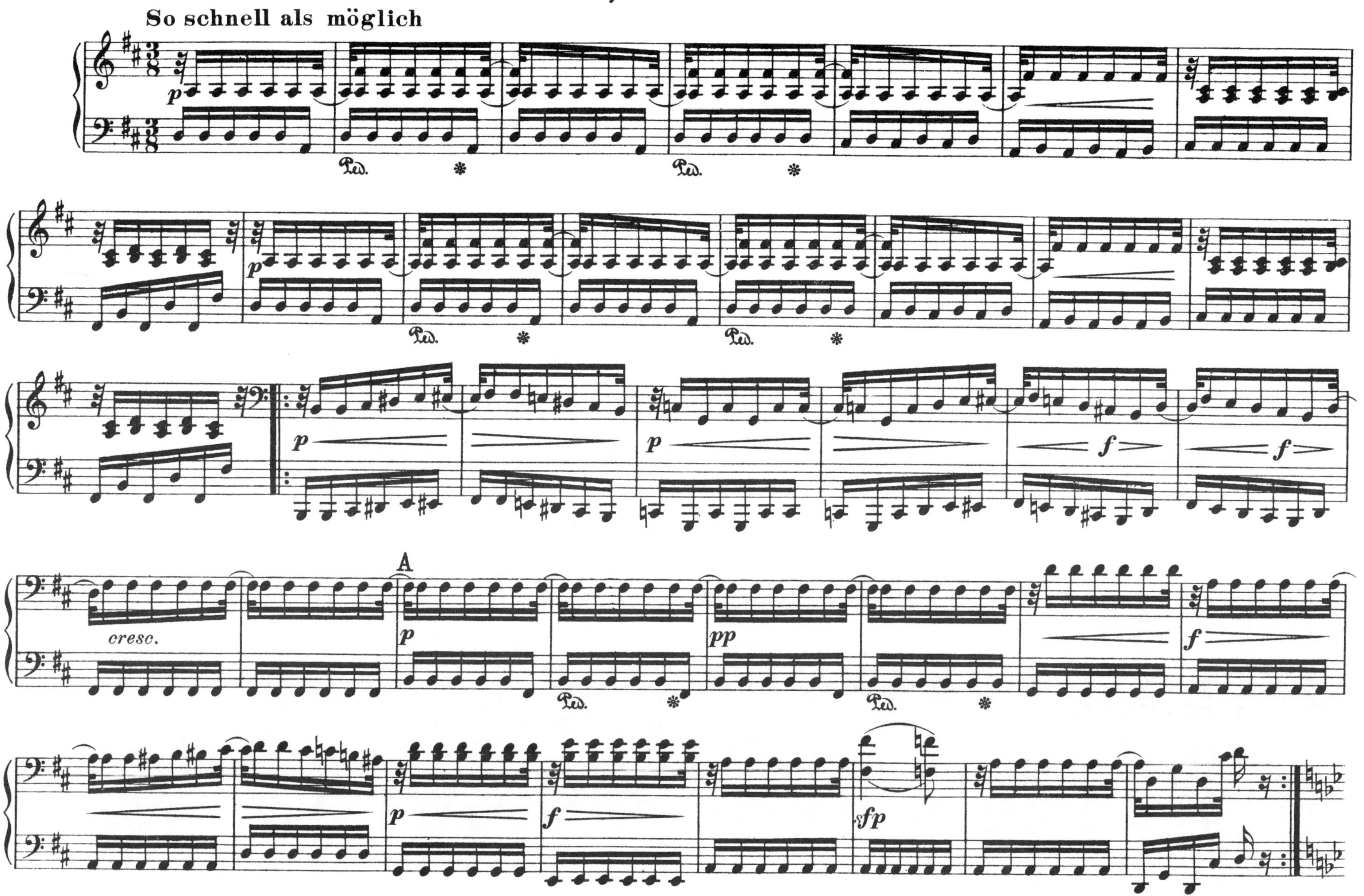

9. By the Fountain

pp
(Mit Verschiebung)
pp
B
ppp
1
pp
Ped.
C
p
Ped.
Ped.

pp
(Mit Verschiebung.)
B
ppp
Ped.
C
p
Ped.
Ped.

p
p
f
f
cresc.
p
pp
Ped.
Ped.
f
p
f
fp
D
p
sf
sf
p

8
p
f
f
cresc.
p
pp
Ped.
Ped.
f
p
f
D
p
8
sf
sf
p

10. Hide-and-Seek

10. Hide-and-Seek

C
D
E
1mo

C
D
E
p
fp
sfz
sf
pp
1

11. Ghost Story

11. Ghost Story

f
ff
sf
D
E
p

f
f
f
f
ff
sf
sf
D
sf
E
f
f
f
f
ff
sf
sf
p

1mo
p
f
f
f
f
p
F
sf
cresc.
f
ff
G
sf
sf
sf
sf
sf
sf
p
H
sf
cresc.
sf
sf
p

mf
sf
sf
f
f
f
f
p
F
cresc.
f
ff
G
sf
sf
sf
sf
H
sf
p
cresc.
sf
sf
p

12. Evening Song

12. Evening Song

To Fräulien Henriette Reichmann in Hull

Ballroom Scenes

9 Character Pieces, Op. 109 (1851)

1. Prelude

To Fräulien Henriette Reichmann in Hull

Ballroom Scenes

9 Character Pieces, Op. 109 (1851)

1. Prelude

f
f
p
cresc.
f
ff
sf
sf
f
B
p
sf
f
f
f
f
sf
sf
f
f
f
sf
f

sf
sf
p
cresc.
f
sf
sf
f
B
p
f
f
f
sf
sf
f
f
f
sf
f

2. Polonaise

2. Polonaise

Nicht zu schnell
f
fp
p
sfp
f
p
f
sf
A
f
f
p
cresc.
f
f
p
sfp
B
sfp
f
p
f
sf

TRIO
p
1.
2.
C
f
f
D
p
f
sfp

TRIO
p
1.
2.
C
f
D
p
f
f
f
fp

p
sfp
f
p
f
sf
E
f
f
p
cresc.
f
sf
f
sf
p
sfp
F
sfp
f
p
f
sf
G
f

p
sfp
f
p
f
sf
E
f
f
p
cresc.
f
f
p
sfp
F
sfp
f
p
f
sf
G
f

3. Waltz

Mäßiges Tempo

3. Waltz

D
4. Hungarian Dance
Lebhaft
A

D
p
f
f
4. Hungarian Dance
Lebhaft
sf
sf
mf
f
sf
sf
A
p
f
p
f
f
p
sf
sf
p

B
C

B
C

p
cresc.
1.
2.
D
f
f
E
ff
p
ff
p
cresc.
F
f
ff

p
cresc.
D
f
8
E
ff
p
ff
p
cresc.
F
f
ff

5. French Dance

5. French Dance

C
D
Schneller

C
D
Schneller

6. Mazurka

6. Mazurka

Sehr markiert

A

B
C

f
sfz
sf
sfz
sf
sf
B
p
f
C
f
p
f
sf
sf
p
sf
sf
7
sf
sf f f
f
sf

D
E
F
Schneller

D
E
F
Schneller.

7. Ecossaise

Lebhaft, nicht zu schnell

7. Ecossaise

D
CODA
E

D

CODA

E

8. Waltz

8. Waltz

p
C
mf
f
sf
sf
sf
D
1
p
f
p
1.
2.
p
E
fp
fp
f
f
p
f
f
p
f
p
p
fp
fp
f
f
p
f
f

C
D
E
1.
2.

p
f
p
f
p
f
F
sf
sf
sf
1
p
ff
G
sf
sf
sf
sf
sf
sf
sf
H

9. Promenade

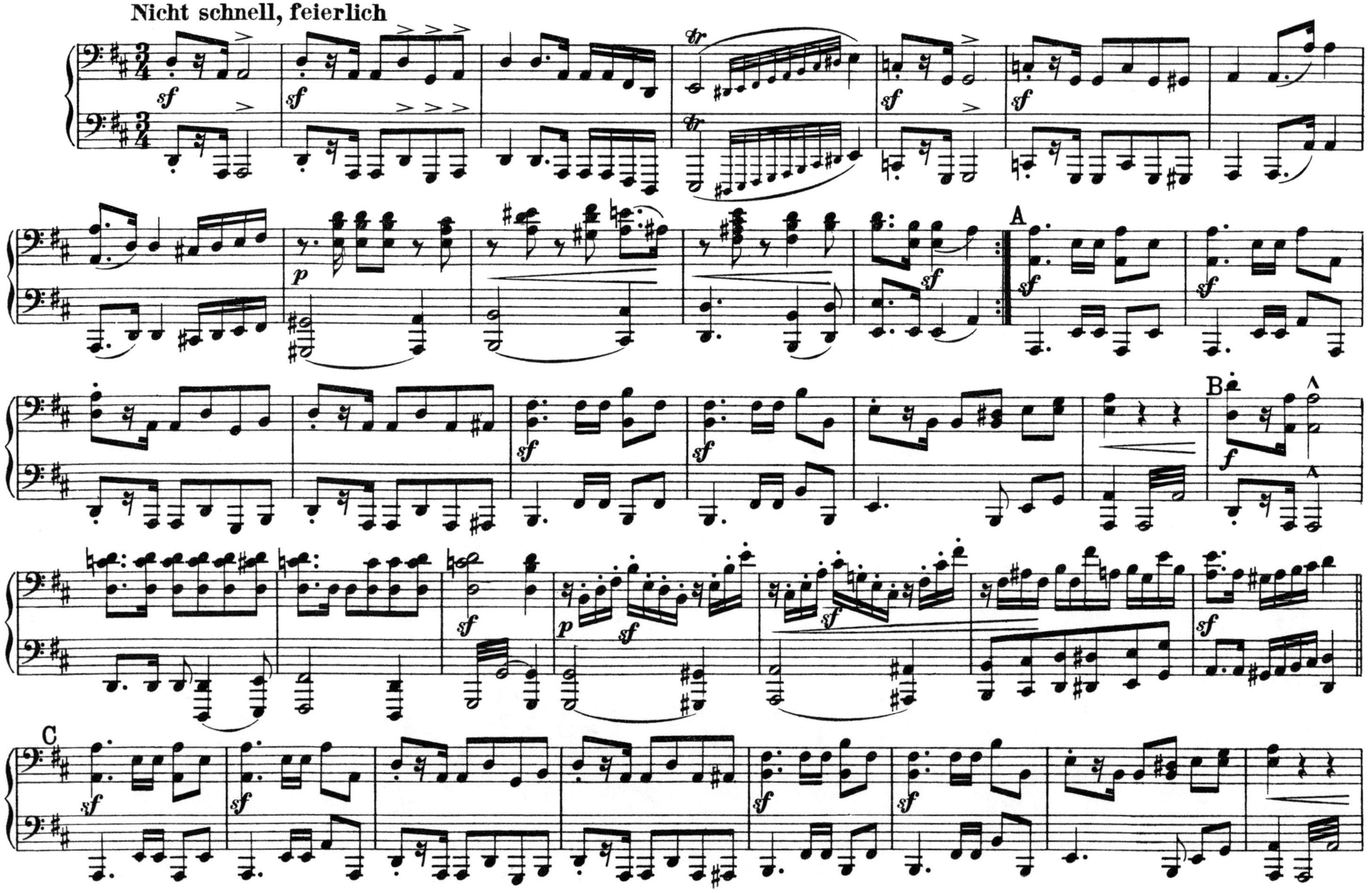
Nicht schnell, feierlich
sf
tr
p
A
B
f
C

9. Promenade

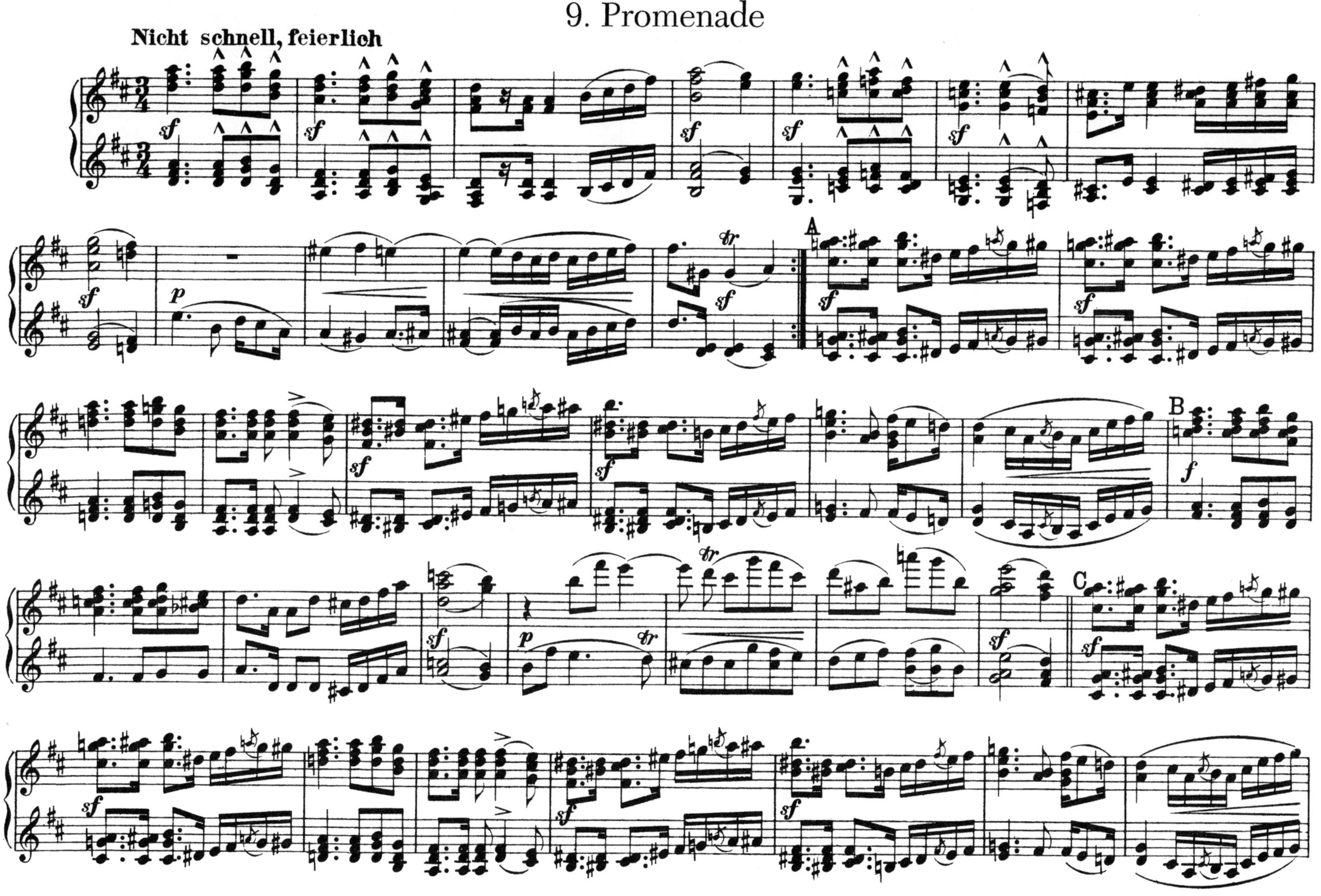
Nicht schnell, feierlich
sf
p
A
B
C
f

f
sf
p
D
1.
2.
E
fp
F
ff
tr

f
sf
p
tr
sf
D
p
1.
2.
E
fp
tr
7
3
1.
2.
ff
F
sf
sf
sf
sf
sf
sf
p
tr
sf

sf
sf
sf
sf
f
sf
p
sf
sf
sf
G
ff
p
f
sf
sf
sf
sf
p
f
ff
sf
Fine

sf
f
p
tr
G
ff
Fine

Children's Ballroom

6 Easy Dance Pieces, Op. 130 (1853)

1. Polonaise

Langsam und gemessen

Secondo

TRIO

Children's Ballroom

6 Easy Dance Pieces, Op. 130 (1853)

1. Polonaise

1.
2.
A
f
sf
tr
B
f
sf
p

1.
2.
A
f
sf
tr
B
f
sf
p
tr
tr

2. Waltz

2. Waltz

3. Minuet

Nicht schnell, etwas gravitätisch

3. Minuet

4. Ecossaise

4. Ecossaise

5. French Dance

Belebt, doch nicht zu rasch

5. French Dance

6. Round Dance

6. Round Dance

p
f
p
f
f
C
sf
p
sf
D
cresc.
mf
f
f
mf
f
f

p
f
p
f
f
C
sf
p
sf
D
cresc.
mf
f
f
mf
f
f

p
cresc.
f
sfp
cresc.
E
f
sf

p
cresc.
f
sfp
cresc.
E
f
sf
Fine